Take This Job and Love It!

My Personal Journey from Full-Time Ministry into Full-Time Work

Tim Strecker, Ph.D.

WESTBOW
PRESS
A DIVISION OF THOMAS NELSON

WestBow Press books may be ordered through booksellers or by contacting:

WestBow Press
A Division of Thomas Nelson
1663 Liberty Drive
Bloomington, IN 47403
www.westbowpress.com
1 (866) 928-1240

Because of the dynamic nature of the Internet, any web addresses or links contained in this book may have changed since publication and may no longer be valid. The views expressed in this work are solely those of the author and do not necessarily reflect the views of the publisher, and the publisher hereby disclaims any responsibility for them.

Any people depicted in stock imagery provided by Thinkstock are models, and such images are being used for illustrative purposes only.
Certain stock imagery © Thinkstock.

ISBN: 978-1-4908-1044-7 (sc)

Library of Congress Control Number: 2013917801

Printed in the United States of America.

WestBow Press rev. date: 10/3/2013

I dedicate this book to the one person who has helped me the most on this exciting and incredible journey, Connie, the love of my life.

Table of Contents

Foreword

This is the story of my personal journey from being a missionary to being an engineer. It is a story of my dreams, my struggles to understand God's calling on my life, and realizing that God places desires in our hearts that are confused many times with our own desires. Growing up I heard pastors and missionaries say many times that the highest calling an individual could have was going into full time ministry. This was reinforced by parents who shared the same belief. So, naturally, I viewed people in full time ministry as God's "elite", the really "chosen" ones and I wanted to be one of them too. Don't get me wrong, there is a need for people in full time ministry and the sacrifices they make and commitment they have is commendable. They aren't the only "called" or "chosen" ones, though, in God's eyes and I think intellectually most believers feel that way, but the way our church life is walked out many times leaves laypeople feeling less significant compared to our full time brothers and sisters. I have also come to understand that pastors and missionaries are in those vocations because they have a passion for it, so, naturally, they are going to want others to pursue full time ministry and encourage it up from the pulpit. It is, many times, the only life they know and understand. But one thing I have never heard from a full time minister was that God might be calling me to work a full time job. In all the years attending church I have never heard a church member get up and give a testimony about how God was leading them to be a mechanic, or dental hygienist, or an engineer like me. It was always a testimony of how God was calling them into full time ministry as a missionary or pastor. I don't think pastors consciously squelched such testimonies; it just wasn't on their radar.

This story highlights how I came to grips with the mistaken idea that a calling to full time work was somehow less significant than a calling to full time ministry. It also highlights how God leads many times by what we think are our own desires which are really from Him and through circumstances that we think are just coincidences. Read on and be encouraged that whether you work full time or are in ministry full time each is equally significant in God's eyes.

Childhood Dreams of Far-Away Places

Early Impressionable Years

I grew up in the beautiful Northwest in the north Seattle area. My dad was a high school teacher and my mom was a home maker with five kids. My parents were committed Christians and raised us to know and love Jesus. My dad had come to know the Lord toward the end of WWII while in the Navy as a result of a Navy buddy sharing the gospel with him. My mom made a commitment to Jesus as a child as she was raised in a Christian home. They both had hearts for the Lord and His work and made sure that the family they raised would be exposed to as much of God's work as possible. Wherever we lived, mom would organize a neighborhood children's Bible school at our house during the summer. She made it a point to share Jesus with all of our friends if they didn't know Him. She provided a great role model for being a missionary wherever you are. Dad taught Sunday school and made sure we attended church three times a week. We almost felt like we had backslidden if we skipped a Sunday evening service to watch the weekly Wonderful World of Disney. But that is the environment I was raised in and thought that was the norm.

I made a commitment to Jesus as a very young child. My parents led each of us to the Lord as soon as we could understand what that meant. I was around 4 years old when my mom had me pray to accept Jesus into my heart. I really did not comprehend all of what I had prayed and it would be many years later in my late teens before I would make a total commitment to the Lord. But, I knew who Jesus was and wanted Him to come into my heart and that was good enough for me at the tender age of four.

King's Garden

I went to elementary school at a Christian school in north Seattle at what is now Christa Ministries, but was then called King's Garden. My dad was a high school teacher at King's Garden, so I attended the elementary school. It was a great place and the teachers were fantastic. Every month we would have an assembly at the big auditorium at the adjacent high school and many times we would have special speakers from the mission field. To get to the auditorium, we would go through an underground tunnel connecting the buildings together. There were a lot of tunnels at King's Garden and we heard rumors that they were built during WWII just in case there were any air raids. Whether this was true or not we never found out, but it made for interesting stories for us boys who liked to play army at lunch.

I think it was when I was in 2nd or 3rd grade that I have my first memory of a missionary speaker who showed slides of their work in India and I was captivated by the idea of someone being able to go to a completely different culture and make an impact on people's lives for Jesus. Missionary speakers would many times want to know if any of us were interested in or felt called to the mission field and would provide a time at the end of the assembly for those who wanted to come forward for prayer. I never raised my hand because I didn't really think I was called to the mission field, though going overseas did interest me.

My family attended church every week where we were also exposed to missionaries traveling through and sharing about their work overseas. So, I had a lot of experiences growing up in my elementary school years with hearing and seeing what God was doing around the world with common people like me. Besides the continual flow of visiting missionaries at church and school, we often heard sermons on the great commission.

The idea of becoming a missionary had entered my mind off and on and was many times in conjunction with the ebb and flow of emphasis at church and school, so a later decision as a young adult to get involved with a short-term missions organization did not seem like an impulsive decision when it finally happened. As I mentioned before, though, I never felt a "call" to missions even when I eventually did go. It was based primarily on a desire to serve God anywhere I could and for a short time that ended up being in several places overseas.

Influence of Music and Science

Music became a big part of my life growing up. My mom loved music and had the radio on and played records (LP's—remember those?!) all the time. She had a beautiful voice and I always enjoyed hearing her sing at home and at church. Whenever one of us kids showed an interest in music or musical instruments she would do everything in her power to make sure we had a chance to attend a musical concert or play an instrument. I got to attend many symphony orchestra concerts after my mom found out about my love for classical music. The creativity of a symphony to make such beautiful music with so many different instruments always intrigued and fascinated me. Later in life this creative side of me would play a larger role in my professional working life, but at the time I saw it as just the love of music. I don't remember what sparked my interest in violin, but I started learning to play the violin when I was eight years old. I played violin for seven years and had dreams of becoming a concert violinist when I grew up. I was sort of a strange kid because I read biographies of many of the well known classical composers such as Beethoven, Mozart, and Bach throughout elementary school years. I guess other kids saw me as strange too just because I played the violin. I had the opportunity of playing in a youth symphony one summer as a 6th grader. It was a lot of fun and also a lot work. Once I got into junior high and high school I gravitated to the guitar which became an instrument I would play throughout adulthood. I would end up playing in worship teams for many years and God has used music in my life to a far greater extent than He used me in formal "missions" work.

Just as my mom was a great influence in my life regarding music, my dad was a great influence in my life regarding the love of science. He was a biology and physical science teacher in high school, so we would always hear about the stuff he was teaching his students at school during dinner many times. He would go into details of photosynthesis or what the cell structure in our body is or about our solar system. These dinner time science lessons would instill a lasting impression and desire to know and understand more of what God created around us. Dad was also a great resource when working on science fair projects. I remember building a working model of an elevator when I was in middle school and dad was there to help me through it. I built it mostly out of wood and it was hand operated, but I learned all about ropes and pulleys that I hadn't known much about before that. It wasn't very elegant looking but it was fun to actually get it to work. My brother and I were always building things like model airplanes and cars, tree houses, and go-carts. We were tinkerers and liked learning about new things. As I look back, music and science have been a big part of my life and God has used them to direct my life in ways I would never dream of. More on that later.

Just before I began junior high we moved to a town east of Everett, Washington, called Lake Stevens. My dad had taken a new teaching position in the neighboring town of Granite Falls since the higher salary provided more for his growing family. It was my first experience of going to a public school and being confronted with non-Christian students. The first year was pretty difficult because I was still playing violin and the continual harassment made me long for the days at my old school at King's Garden. I played violin in the junior high band for one year. I stopped after that year because private violin lessons had ended due to financial strains and I lost my motivation to continue playing violin. About a year later I became interested in the guitar and I bought a used acoustic guitar. This would start my life-long love of the guitar.

Throughout junior high and high school I played guitar in school bands, both regular big bands and jazz bands. A couple of friends and I tried starting a rock and roll band but nothing became of it. We just got together and made a lot of noise, but it was fun trying to be creative and learn how to play with small group of musicians without a conductor that I was used to in bands and orchestras.

It was during my high school years that I abandoned my faith in God. I did not reject God but it was more that I was rebelling against my parents and since they believed in God that got included in my rebellion. Though I still attended church, my heart was not in it. Right after I graduated from high school I moved in with a high school buddy who had his own place. His parents had moved out and sold him the house. What a novel idea! It was during this time that I recommitted myself to the Lord.

My First Tech Industry Job

I was working as an electronics technician at an aerospace electronics company just south of Everett at the time I moved in at my high school friend's place. I had gone to a community college and studied 2 years to get an associate's degree in electronics. I really enjoyed the job and there were so many interesting things to learn and experience. One of the things I worked on was part of a heads-up display used on F14 fighter jets. These heads-up displays allowed a fighter pilot to see data and information displayed right in front of him on the cockpit glass windshield that he looked out of while flying. One day an engineer and I were working on a problem with part of the system and as we were staring at a circuit board on the test bench in front of us one of the capacitors blew up sending paper confetti all over us and the bench. Both of us jumped back and let out a yell from being startled, but neither of us was injured from it. It sounded like firecracker going off and produced about the same affect. We had a good laugh after we recovered and found out it was the capacitor which was causing the problem in the first place. It had been put in the circuit board backwards, causing it to heat up and, eventually, blow up. This was my first job working in a scientific based profession and I found it fascinating. I marveled at how engineers had figured out how to use electrons to make useful things such as heads-up displays or TVs or stereos and my job allowed me to take what the engineers had designed and to make it work along with fixing any problems it had. It was also my first exposure to a manufacturing environment and seeing how products are mass produced using modern manufacturing processes and techniques. I really enjoyed my job and found I was also good at doing it.

Dreaming of Europe

There were five of us living in my friend's house and one Sunday afternoon some of my house mates and I were looking at maps of Europe. One of us mentioned how fun it would be to travel around Europe before any of us got tied down with spouses and family. We decided to start planning for a European trip the following year. By the time we needed to start getting serious about saving for the trip and purchasing gear for bicycling across Europe (we had decided by then that bicycling was the way we wanted to see Europe), everyone but myself dropped out. One house mate, Dan, who owned the house decided he wanted to go and since he was the only other one besides me that had a full time job, I felt he would be the most likely to succeed in going with me. Though the others really had the desire to go, they did not have jobs that paid enough for them to save for the trip. So, Dan and I started our yearlong effort of planning and saving for our European trip that would be life changing in many respects.

Across Europe on a Bicycle

Long Hair and True Love

During the year of planning I met and started dating my future wife, Connie. We met at the house I lived at with Dan and the other house mates because we had weekly youth group meetings in the basement where sometimes up to a hundred young people would congregate for singing and Bible study. Connie came one week with a friend of hers I knew who introduced Connie to me. What initially attracted me so much to Connie, along with her good looks, was her waist length hair. She was and still is a beautiful and attractive woman! At first I thought Connie was a lot younger than she was so I was reluctant to ask her out, but her friend assured me that she was not that much younger so I did ask her out and never regretted it! Our first date was roller skating at a local roller rink. Roller skating was a popular activity back then, though now a days it is not very common. We enjoyed our time together and started dating regularly. I did let her know after we started dating that Dan and I were planning a European trip in which we initially planned to be gone for a year. Connie seemed to be intrigued by our trip and initially seemed genuinely interested about it, but I could tell that as our departure date grew closer that she was not as excited about it. By the time Dan and I left for Europe, Connie and I had been dating for about six months. Connie sent me many letters during the six months I was in Europe. I had quite a stack of perfume-scented letters by the time I came back home. But, I'm getting ahead of myself!

Why Did We Go to Europe?

Dan and I didn't plan this trip with any real spiritual purpose in mind like evangelism or outreach per se, but we were open to the idea if it sprang up. The primary purpose in our minds at the time was to see a bigger part of the world and do it while we were still young and able. Neither of us had traveled internationally before so we had a very U.S. centric view of the world around us and we yearned to see the broader picture of what God was up to in other parts of the world. We were definitely interested in seeing what God was doing in His church in Europe and we regularly attended services and youth groups while traveling when there was an opportunity.

Midnight Sun and Northern Hospitality

Dan and I initially traveled to Bergen, Norway in June of 1977. Dan knew a family in Bergen and he arranged for us to stay there for a couple of months prior to starting our bike trip through the rest of Europe. A small island near Bergen, called Askoy, was where the family actually lived. It was a short 15 minute ferry trip from downtown Bergen to Askoy and then about a 20 minute walk to the family's home. There was no public transportation and the family we were staying with didn't have a car we could use so we either walked or bicycled to see things. Askoy is approximately at the same latitude as Anchorage, Alaska so they have long summer nights where it never really gets dark. The island is lightly populated and very peaceful. It is about 15 miles long and 5 miles across at its widest spot. We spent many days exploring the island on bicycle. The island is mostly rolling meadows with sparse trees and a rocky coastline. The summer was fairly warm where the day time temperatures could reach the mid 70s.

The family we stayed with showed us great Norwegian hospitality. Food was always at the center of family activities. For breakfast we learned to eat toast with cheese and jam instead of butter and jam. Norwegian white cheese is very mild and tastes great with jam on it. Eggs and meat slices were also part of the breakfast menu. Lunches consisted of open-faced sandwiches eaten with a fork and knife, cutting them into bite-sized pieces and then using the fork to get it to our mouth. Fish was a main staple at dinner time as were other meats like pork and beef. Boiled potatoes and vegetables were served along with the main course. We did try lutefisk a couple of times but never developed a taste for it. After dinner guests would often stop by three to four days a week since it was a novelty to have American guests visiting for an extended period of time. The living room coffee table became the dessert tray loaded with all kinds of mouth-watering treats from cookies and cakes to pastries and cobblers. One of my favorite desserts was fruit with heavy cream poured over it and eaten with a spoon. Coffee and tea were always served with dessert. Our surrogate family spoiled us beyond words. For a couple of guys in our early 20s with an endless appetite we thought we had already arrived in heaven!

During our 2 month stay in Askoy we did a lot of bicycling to get in shape for our upcoming trip. We also did a lot of reading. We read through the entire Bible during our time in Askoy, in about 6 weeks. It was great to read it in entirety in such a short time. We didn't read to study it in depth but to get the big picture. It was the first time I had read through the Bible in my life and in such a short time. It started a pattern in my life of reading through the Bible once a year for many years.

We did not do any traveling beyond Askoy and Bergen that summer as we knew we would be traveling a lot soon by bicycle across Europe. We wanted to absorb as much of the Norwegian culture as we could with our family in Askoy. It turned out to be one of the things we remembered and cherished the most in our memories about Europe.

Broken Spokes and Peddling Downhill

Our summer in Norway passed quickly and by the end of August we were preparing for our bicycle trip in earnest. We had bought the Raleigh ten speed touring bikes, camping equipment, and panniers before coming to Europe. We planned to camp as much as possible and stay at hostels when there were no camp sites available to cut costs. We said our goodbyes to our surrogate family on Askoy and headed east to Oslo, our first planned stop of the trip. We had about 60 pounds of equipment and supplies loaded on our bikes and the first problem we encountered was breaking wheel spokes. We soon found out that the wheels needed to be adjusted so that all the spokes were the same tension to prevent future breaks. On our trip to Oslo from Bergen we had to go over a mountain range. It was so steep on the western slope that we ended up pushing our bikes up much of the mountain. We were anticipating a much needed rest by coasting down the eastern slope of the mountain. What we were confronted with was a stiff head wind and a much more gradual descent so we ended up having to pedal all the way down the mountain! It was a little over 300 miles from Bergen to Oslo and we were doing about 40-50 miles a day. We had not been training with any weight on our bikes so we were not riding as many miles a day as we had anticipated. We stayed in Oslo for a few days with some friends of the family in Askoy. Then we headed off for Jonkoping, Sweden about 250 miles away. Jonkoping is at the southern end of Lake Vattern, the second largest lake in Sweden. The roads in Sweden were much better than in Norway since they were better condition and flatter terrain. The tractor-trailer rigs were also much bigger. We could feel ourselves being slightly pulled towards a truck as it went by us on the road from the suction it created. It was a little unnerving at first, but we got used to it. As we neared Jonkoping the freeways became a lot busier and harder to navigate on bicycles. We met a truck driver at a rest stop and asked him if he could take us and our bikes into Jonkoping and he agreed. It was the only time on our bike trip that we did this. Dan's Norwegian family had some friends in Jonkoping who we stayed with during our weeklong visit. This was our first and only opportunity to interact much with a church. There were several reasons for this. One is that we had contacts there; a second reason is that most of the young people spoke very good English, and lastly, this particular church had a lot of activities going on all week long for young people. When they found out we both played guitar and sang they asked us do a few songs for their large youth group meetings one evening for several hundred young people. It was a lot of fun. Dan and I had played a lot together so we had some songs we knew really well. This part of Sweden was experiencing a spiritual renewal and we could tell that the young people were very excited about their spiritual lives and wanted to go deeper with God. It was a very invigorating experience for us and was one of the highlights of our trip.

From Jonkoping we headed for Helsingborg where we took a short ferry ride to Denmark. We went to Copenhagen for a few days and then on to Kiel, Germany. From Kiel we rode to Bremen where we had a funny experience. We had located a camp ground on our map and were trying to reach it before it got dark. When we got to the spot there was no camp ground there. So we decided to continue to ride until we found a suitable spot to set up our tent for the night. We finally found a quiet field, set up tent, and went to sleep. We were awakened early in the morning with sounds of cars and traffic very close to us. We peered out our tent to see that we had camped in the middle of a circular on ramp to the autobahn! Needless to say we packed up quickly and got out of there before the local police showed up to find out why we were there. From there we headed for Emmen, The Netherlands about a 120 miles west of Bremen. We tried to steer clear of large cities and traveled country roads as much as possible. In doing this it was a lot nicer and we got to see the many small towns and villages along the way. We usually got up in the morning, packed up, and rode to the nearest town to get breakfast from a local grocery store. We did the same for lunch and dinner. We ate a lot of locally baked breads, cuts of meat, cheese, and fruit. We always enjoyed the many local bakeries where we would feast on baked goodies.

Belgium Waffles and German Castles

We traveled along the eastern side of The Netherlands and Belgium. We actually had a Belgium waffle in Belgium! We were riding through the rural country side of Belgium in the pouring down rain in late September. It was a cold day and the rain was not letting up. We saw a road-side café up ahead so we stopped to have some lunch and get warmed up. The café had a nice warm fire burning in the fireplace. We asked the waiter if they served Belgium waffles and he said they did. So, we ordered waffles and hot coffee and sat by the fire to warm up while we ate. It was really difficult to leave that warm café to get back on our wet bikes and ride on in a cold rain. From Belgium we rode into Luxembourg where we stayed for about a week. It was at this point that we decided that it was time to stop our bike trip since the weather was getting colder and wetter. We had ridden approximately 1200 miles in six weeks. We bought train tickets back to Bergen, Norway, loaded our bikes and equipment onto the train and headed back to our family in Askoy. We stayed in Askoy for about two weeks and then purchased Interail train tickets for unlimited train travel in Europe. We saw the rest of Europe by rail including the UK and one eastern block country, then called Yugoslavia. While in southern Germany we stayed at a missionary base of Youth With A Mission (YWAM) at an old small castle in Bavaria. It was in the small town of Hurlach. We stayed there for a week. It was another highlight of our trip. We attended classes where YWAM teachers taught in English.

We ate and fellowshipped with many young people our age who were on fire for God and wanted to see His purposes fulfilled in the world through their lives. It was our first exposure to YWAM and it would be a deciding factor in my life of eventually working with YWAM in the U.S. YWAM is a short-term mission's organization for young people to get exposure to other cultures and missionary type work. YWAM has Discipleship Training Schools like the one we attended at the German castle where students spend 3 months learning about things such as the character of God, spiritual warfare, and many other topics. After the school phase there is a 3 month outreach, evangelism phase where students learn how to reach out and share their faith with others. We left the YWAM base after a week full of excitement about what God was doing and what opportunities might be in store for the future in short term missions. From there we traveled to Switzerland, Austria, Italy, Yugoslavia, Spain, France, England, and Scotland. We usually stayed a few days to a week in each location. We ended our travels where we started: in Askoy, Norway with our surrogate family. We spent our last couple of weeks in Askoy before flying back home arriving just before Thanksgiving. It had been an exciting and busy 6 month adventure in Europe. It had also been a time when we were exposed to different cultures, ideas, and seeing a bigger picture of what God was doing in the world. It was also a time where I began to ask God if He was leading me into full time missions work at some point.

Into Full-Time Ministry—Finally!

God's Voice Sounds A Lot Like My Wife's

I went back to work after the holidays in January 1978 at the aerospace electronics manufacturing company I had been working at as an electronics technician south of Everett prior to our European trip. I was excited to be home and get re-acquainted with my girlfriend Connie. I had carried her stack of perfumed letters with me all over Europe and now they were with me back home. I was as excited to see her as she was to see me and we picked up where we left off six months earlier. A year and a half later we were married and we settled into our new life together both working at the same aerospace electronics company. Connie worked on one of the manufacturing lines and I still worked as a technician. During our first year of marriage we talked a lot about God's plans for us as a couple. We wanted to do something for Him and felt that full time ministry might be an option. I had found a YWAM base in Tacoma, WA about an hour and half south of where we lived and we started praying about whether we should get involved with them. I had fond memories of the week I spent at the Bavarian YWAM base and had a desire to work with them full time Lord willing. We decided that we would wait until we had been married a year before making any decisions about YWAM. As we approached the first anniversary of our marriage I began to press Connie about it as I felt hesitancy on her part to join YWAM. I am a head strong person and I continued to bug Connie until she finally agreed to join YWAM in February of 1980. This would come back to haunt me many times in the coming years. God had placed Connie in my life to chip away the head strong behavior and become more sensitive and a listener to both God's voice and her's. But as a new husband and immature believer I believed I had "heard" God on this one and that she should just submit and follow me into full time missions. Well, she did follow me but whether she submitted or not is another story. She was not rebellious or verbally telling me "no way!", but she did let me know in subtle ways that she was not going to be a full time missionary her entire life. God would use my wife in a big way to lead us out of full time ministry back into the working world, but at the time I was ignoring His promptings through her.

Tacoma, Edmonton, and the Atomic Bomb

We went through YWAM's six month training program, Discipleship Training School (DTS), in Tacoma where we heard many great teachers speak on spiritual warfare, the character of God, and other topics. After a 3 month training phase we embarked on a 2 month short term missions trip to Alberta, Canada for evangelism to college students at the University of Alberta in Edmonton and to native America Indians in the Canadian Rockies. We also stopped at many local churches to talk about short term missions and YWAM. We traveled many hundreds of miles in a converted white school bus on this trip to Canada. After we finished our DTS we joined a Mobile Team whose mission was to go out to local churches in the Pacific Northwest and recruit young people for YWAM. We also went on a 2 month short term mission to Saipan and Tinian, two islands north of Guam in the Mariana Islands of which Guam is the southernmost. YWAM had a base on Saipan and we spent our first couple of weeks there. We spent the rest of our time on Tinian evangelizing the people there who believed in a mixture of Catholicism and Animism. Tinian is the island where the B29 bombers were loaded with the atomic bombs which were dropped on Japan in WWII.

Tinian loading site for atomic bomb on B29 in WWII

The people on Saipan and Tinian spoke English so there was no language barrier to overcome, only a religious one. The belief in Animism was much stronger than Catholicism because of the supernatural things they saw. They related how they regularly saw a spirit of a woman who appeared out in the more remote parts of the island. They saw other supernatural manifestations too. To these people, Catholicism was a belief system and Animism was the supernatural. Most people outside of Europe and North America have a much greater appreciation for the supernatural as the Tinian people did, but most don't associate Christianity with the supernatural. We had heard many stories during our DTS teaching phase of missionaries who experienced the power of God to show people like those on Tinian the supernatural acts of God. In one instance in the Marshall Islands in the south Pacific, a witch doctor pronounced a spell on a chicken and it dropped dead. The missionary countered the spell with God's power and brought the chicken back to life! That got the islander's attention and showed them that God's power is real and is stronger than a witch doctor's. Seldom do us believers in America see and experience God's power in this way. We have a more rational view of God, not a supernatural one. A lot of believers in the rest of the world expect to see God's power manifested. The Tinian trip helped me to understand this in a clearer way.

Ministry on a Shoe String

Relationship Financing

One of the things we learned while in YWAM was to trust God for finances. YWAM operates as many missions' organizations do which require the people who join them to raise their own monthly support. We had always heard growing up in church that God provides for all that we have but we had usually seen this through finding a job and receiving a paycheck. Depending on God to provide when you don't see where the money is coming from is entirely another matter. What we came to realize is that God provides money through people, not out of the clear blue sky. Most of the time the money came from people we knew, but there were a few instances where we received money anonymously through the mail. We approached our church we were members of in Lake Stevens about supporting us. We were very involved in the church before going into missions so there was a relationship and trust already established when we asked them to support us. They were very interested in missions and having one of their "own" going into missions was very exciting for them. They supported us the entire time we were in YWAM. It was a great partnership. We also had many individuals such as family and friends who supported us. It was a faith-builder seeing how God provided for our growing family living on a shoe-string budget compared to the average American. We were below the poverty level as far as income goes, though food and housing were provided.

Not Poor Church Mice

When we first joined YWAM we had a few hundred dollars support each month. The first six months training we had already paid for before joining up which included room and board so our expenses weren't really that great. After the training was completed, though, we had to begin thinking more seriously about how we were going to pay for our monthly support we required if we were going to continue to work with YWAM. As I mentioned earlier, we approached our church, family, and friends for support. We sent out a monthly newsletter which highlighted the work we were involved in. By the time we left YWAM we had a monthly support of almost $800 per month. This level of support was very rarely seen in the rank and file of YWAM. Most of the staff and trainees in YWAM were barely getting by.

God's Favor

Both of our children were born while we were in YWAM in Tacoma. Health care was a lot cheaper 30 years ago compared to today, but we still had to trust God to provide for us since we didn't have any insurance. Leah and Luke were both healthy babies and we believed it was God's provision of good health that prevented many doctor bills while they were growing up. When we eventually went back to school and the working world we continued to trust God for our finances and health that we had learned to do while in full time ministry. Full time ministry taught us to never take God's provision for granted whether it was through supporters or through an employer. We understood that it was ultimately God who provided a job and granted favor with an employer. It was God who gave me the ability to go back to school at age 26 to get a bachelor's degree in engineering after being out of high school for 8 years. I read the story of Daniel in the Old Testament with new understanding seeing that he was in a high position in the Babylonian government because of God's favor on his life and giving him the ability to excel in knowledge above his peers. The same favor and God-given ability was seen in Jacob's life in Egypt serving in the second highest government position in Pharaoh's kingdom. Another example is of Ruth. She gained favor of the king to rescue her people in his pagan kingdom. If it wasn't for God's favor she and her people would have died. As working believers, why shouldn't we approach our jobs the same way as these people did? Why shouldn't we believe for God's favor with our bosses and co-workers and for the ability to excel in knowledge above our peers? God's people should be the smartest and greatest people to work with in the world!

The Professor from Heaven

The Galloping Gourmet and Higher Education

While on the Mobile Team we got to know a group of people working at YWAM in Tacoma who were using appropriate technology for meeting the practical needs of people in developing countries. They called themselves Tentmaker Ministries based on apostle Paul's model of being a tentmaker to support his ministry. It was headed by Graham Kerr, the former Galloping Gourmet hit TV show host years earlier. Graham and his wife, Treena, had met the Lord and then joined YWAM. They had come up with ideas for more efficient outdoor ovens and composting methods. They had also worked on developing tools that local people in rural areas could use without need of power or engines to drive them. They and their team developed expertise in appropriate technologies to meet the needs of under developed countries and as a way to gain access to those countries that many times wouldn't allow a missionary to come but would allow tentmakers. It was exciting stuff. They had outside speakers come in all the time and one of them was a professor from Purdue University who taught on alternative agriculture practices geared for under developed countries. I had been sensing a growing desire of going back to school over a year's period of time but my thoughts were more on Bible school rather than a secular university. I had even applied to a one year Bible school in Pasadena at the U.S. Center for World Missions. But when I applied to attend the next year the school was shut down. I joked about how God had to close the school down to keep me out! Whether this is true or not is not the point, but it did get me thinking that maybe I was looking at the wrong type of school. I decided to make an appointment with the professor from Purdue to get his perspective. He opened my eyes to the possibilities of using a trade or profession as a means to reach people who are unreachable to regular missionaries. At first I was not too excited because I just wanted to get out there and do something for God, not spend years going to school to get an education and training. I was too vital to God's plan for evangelizing the world to get bogged down in mundane things like studying and taking exams. People were dying and going to hell by the thousands each day so how could I justify going to school when more pressing things were at hand! What arrogance and naivety on my part. God was more than capable of getting the job done without my help. He was more concerned about my character and relationship with Him than what I could "do" for Him. But, that would take another few years to sink into my thick skull and stubborn will. It was another sign post along the road that God was leading me on to a vocation in engineering.

So, where was God leading me to go to school? And what did He want me to study? How long was I going to have to go to school and sideline my most important mission in life to evangelize the unreached? Answering these questions was going to take several more years and a major re-adjusting of my thinking of what God's plan was for my life. It was going to be a journey that initially was gut wrenching to me but very exciting for Connie because she saw a way out of my pre-occupation with missions and our life of poverty.

Calculus, Physics, and Chemistry, Oh No!

I went to the local community college in Tacoma, WA to talk to an advisor about how many classes it would take to finish an electronic engineering degree. Since I had a two year degree for an electronic technician I assumed it would only take a year or two more to complete a bachelor's degree for electronic engineering. What I found out was that the only class from the electronic technician degree that would count towards a bachelor's degree was English literature class! I was mortified. I didn't want to waste any more time on obtaining a degree than needed but what I found out was that the two year degree I already had only counted for one class. I would basically need to start a bachelor's engineering degree from scratch! I was devastated. What I also found out was that the engineering degree would require more math, chemistry, and physics classes which I had not taken for the technician degree. I was deficient in all these areas, so, in addition to the engineering curriculum, I would need to go back and take all the prerequisite classes for these as well. It would become a lesson in humility and perseverance. I was a married man with two kids who was taking classes with recent high school graduates who had just taken calculus, chemistry, and physics courses in high school. I had never taken any of these courses in high school. So, I was behind the eight ball and had to study twice as hard as these recent high school graduates. But I swallowed my pride and learned from these young students knowing that if I persevered I would make it. It didn't matter how smart a person was, but how hard a person was willing to work to succeed. I saw a lot of very smart students fail primarily due to laziness, not because any lack of smarts. They had done well in high school and thought that college owed them a degree. I was willing to work twice as hard as they did so I ended up doing as well as they did. God was also giving me the ability to learn calculus, chemistry, and physics. I had never taken any of these courses before in high school or community college. It was a confidence builder and confirmed that I was doing what God wanted me to do.

Why Do I feel Like a Second Class Citizen

Being in the Right Place at the Right Time

During the time of transition from full time ministry back to school I continued to struggle with the idea of leaving missions and going back to a "regular" job. I liked missions. I liked the adventure of trusting God to provide for us, working with God to change lives, and impact cultures who had never heard of the good news. I also liked the prestige in the local church for being a missionary, God's elite. People looked up to us and admired our commitment and sacrifice. But I had a nagging feeling that this wasn't going to be the life for me. I had read of missionaries who had taken their families onto the mission field and destroyed their lives and marriages because of a false notion of God's calling to be missionaries. Some might say that they succumbed to the attacks of the enemy on their lives. That may have been true in some cases, but I believe it was many times a case of not being in the right place at the right time. A husband talks his wife in to going on this great adventure called missions and she reluctantly goes with him hoping he will eventually change his mind. This was the case with our family. I bugged Connie until she reluctantly agreed to go for a short term mission with YWAM. Her hope was that once this phase in my life was over that I would come to my senses and get a "real" job! And she had continued to remind me while in YWAM that she wasn't going to do this her entire life. Her family also didn't understand why we were doing this. It made no sense to them why I would drag my family into poverty conditions for the sake of reaching people for God.

Covert Missionaries

So, I was beginning to get a glimpse of how God was using my wife to change my thinking and my decisions about our life's direction. But, I wasn't completely there yet. I had another plan brewing: let's be tentmakers like the apostle Paul or like other professionals today who use their profession to get into closed countries. That's how I justified going back to school in my mind. I was still going to be a missionary, just a "covert" one! So, I changed the terminology from missionary to tentmaker, but not my thinking. I was still going to drag my family to some faraway place whether they liked it or not. As I said earlier, I'm a head strong, stubborn person, so God was going to have to work overtime on me.

The Cambodian Connection

I went to a community college in Tacoma for three years before transferring to Washington State University in Pullman. I continued to be involved with YWAM while attending Tacoma community college. I helped with YWAM's Cambodian refugee ministry which grew out of helping resettle thousands of Cambodian refugees who came to the Puget Sound area after the genocide of Pol Pot in Cambodia. Many of them had spent years in refugee camps in Thailand and Hong Kong before coming to America. They were people from an agrarian society with little education so coming to America was freedom from genocide but challenging to get integrated into our modern society and find jobs. Many depended on federal assistance until they could get trained and find jobs. The younger ones assimilated very quickly but the older people found it difficult and sometimes impossible to find work because of their age and language barriers. YWAM's refugee ministry helped these people find housing, aid, and meet basic needs such as how to shop at a modern grocery store. Most of these people had never been to a grocery store. They had lived on farms where they raised most of their food or gone to a local market where nothing was packaged. When they went to a Safeway or Albertsons they had no idea what to look for. Even buying meat was a challenge because they didn't know the language and the packaged meat didn't look anything like the pig or chicken hanging on a hook in a local Cambodian market or one they had slaughtered to eat on the farm. So imagine the frustration they felt when they couldn't even go grocery shopping without help. The refugees were so grateful for any help we could give them and it was rewarding work in meeting the felt needs they had. I learned how to repair dryers and washers. I also spent many hours at DSHS offices in Tacoma with families who needed assistance. In the back of my mind this was rewarding and meaningful work. It was reaching a people who were unreachable while in Cambodia but God had brought them to our doorstep and they were eager to learn everything American including their "religion". They thought all Americans where Christians but were shocked to find out that many were not. As we spent time helping them we had many opportunities to share the love of God with them. They were eager to listen . . . for a season.

Senders and Goers

The thought of going back to school and work was still a struggle for me. It was so mundane compared to ministering to hurting, needy people. Why would God want me to stop doing such needed ministry to go to school and study for years to prepare for a career that met my family's needs but didn't impact people like these refugees? Again, God still had some work to do to change my thinking.

During this time a book was published addressing the idea of senders and goers. There are those who God wants to go to unreached countries and reach out to the people there. These are the goers. Then, there are those who God wants to stay home, find work, and support those who go. These are the senders. If everyone was a goer there would be no money to support them. There need to be many more senders than goers. Just because a person is a sender doesn't mean they are any less committed to the cause than a goer. It is only a matter of geography, not commitment and passion for the lost. I read this book with great interest and it was another sign post along the road God was leading me that He was using to change my thinking. But, in the mean time, I was still going down the road with the idea that I wanted to be a tentmaker and a goer.

Hitting the Books

Wazzu or Bust

After finishing three years at Tacoma Community College, we packed up and said goodbye to western Washington and headed out to the rolling wheat fields of eastern Washington near the Idaho border. We had grown up in the greener, lusher side of Washington State in the Puget Sound area where Seattle, Tacoma, and Everett nestle next to the quiet waters of Puget Sound between two mountain ranges, the Olympics and the Cascades. Now we would be living in a land-locked place called Pullman where Washington State University (or affectionately known as Wazzu) is located. No water, no mountains, no trees, and hardly any people. We thought this was our "wilderness" experience! Spokane was about 75 miles north of Pullman and we drove up there any chance we had since it was a city about the size of Tacoma and we missed the city. Pullman had only about 11,000 residents not including the students at WSU. We missed western Washington and couldn't wait to finish up my bachelor's degree at WSU and move back there. We had no idea that we would end up staying in Pullman for over eight years and then be moving to the mid-west before finally landing back in the northwest in Oregon. But, I'm getting ahead of myself.

Washington State University, Pullman, WA

A funny story occurred when I applied to transfer to WSU from Tacoma Community College. Once I was accepted at WSU we started to receive advertisements and invitations from fraternities there. We laughed because they had no idea that I had a wife and kids and we joked that we should show up during rush with the "fam" and see the looks on their faces! I had decided that I would pursue a degree in Agricultural Engineering specializing in food processing. I believed that this would be a great avenue to gain access to developing countries as I had learned from the Cambodian refugee stories about the need for improved food supplies. The professor from Purdue who taught at YWAM was a specialist in agriculture so he had an influence on my decision for this degree too.

Drowning in Fluid Mechanics

My first semester at WSU was difficult for a few reasons. One was we were in Pullman! Another was the semester terms at WSU were a lot longer than the quarter terms at the community college. And, lastly, one of the classes I took was brutal. It was a mechanical engineering class in fluid mechanics. It was very interesting but also very demanding. The mid-term exam was one of the worst I ever took in college. And since there were only two exams: a mid-term and final exam, the mid-term was important to do well on. I studied hard for the mid-term. When the prof handed out the exam and I started to look at the questions, I panicked! There were six questions on the exam. As I looked at the first question I had no idea how to solve it. I went to the second question and had no idea how to solve it. I had no idea how to solve any of the questions! So, I went back to each question and just started to write down how I thought it should be solved along with assumptions. Fortunately, most engineering exams are graded not on the correct answer but how you set up the problem, your assumptions, and lastly the numbers. If the problem was set up correctly with the right assumptions but the wrong number was calculated for the answer, you would still get most of the credit since you have the concept down. So, I was going for all the partial credit I could get even if I didn't have a clue how to solve them. When we got our exams back the next week we were all shocked. The exam was worth 100 points. The average was 29 points! So, most of the class scored less than 50 points on a 100 point exam. I got a score of 41 just on partial credits, but it was still a shocker to score so poorly. I was so discouraged! I had never got a score that low on any exam I took at Tacoma Community College. Was the community college too easy on us? Didn't they prepare us for university-level courses?

I was beginning to wonder. But in the end, I did get a B+ in the fluid mechanics course and it gave me confidence I could make it at WSU. I still had a lot of hard courses to take, but I figured if I could survive fluid mechanics, I could pass any course. Fluid mechanics was seen as a weed out class for mechanical engineers and I had survived with the best of them, so I felt that if God wanted me in this degree He was going to give me the ability to learn the material and concepts.

College Educated Tentmakers

We attended a church which had a lot of college students our age and was very missions minded. When they found out we had been in YWAM, we were asked to be involved in their mission's activities in the church which included a missions committee, an annual mission's emphasis week, and other missions-related activities. I also got involved with sponsoring a mission's conference on campus targeted to college students who wanted to use their degree as tentmakers. A lot of the churches in town participated along with their campus ministries. Mission's organizations which emphasized tentmaker missions were asked to come and set up tables and booths at the conference. Hundreds of students attended the conference and were excited to hear about opportunities to use their college education to reach people who were unreachable by traditional missionaries and still get to use their college training to earn a living. It was exciting to see students who had no idea what opportunities existed for them to have their eyes opened to a world looking for people with their training and expertise. I was also hoping that I would find a similar opportunity when I finished my degree. It was during these missions' conferences that I learned about teaching English as a second language in countries around the world. I was interested in

China and so began to look into opportunities for teaching English in universities in China.

Plans Derailed by Tiananmen Square

I finished my bachelor's degree in spring of 1987. I was anxious to finally finish a degree that I initially thought would only take a couple of years, but took over 5 years to complete. One of my professors asked if I would be interested in staying on for a master's degree. We prayed about it and felt God leading us to stay and get the additional degree thinking that this would enhance my chances of teaching English in China, a country that places much emphasis on education. After completing the master's degree in a little over a year we moved back to Tacoma to work at a local food processing company there while preparing to go to China. I worked for the company for six months. We were making plans with an organization who places people in China for teaching English during that six months in Tacoma. We got all of our shots, looked into home schooling curricula for our kids, and got our passports renewed and new ones for the kids. Everything looked like we were headed to China to spend a year or two teaching English until Tiananmen Square massacre changed all of our plans. It was another sign post along the road God was leading me down to show me He had other plans for our family. After Tiananmen Square massacre American families were discouraged in going to China because of the country's instability and volatile conditions. So, reluctantly I refocused and began asking God where He was leading us now. Connie was relieved that we were not taking our young children into unknown conditions and we were now finally not thinking about going to China. Up until that roadblock occurred, I had been pushing to go to China for over four years and had been telling our church and family we were going there. So, with the wind taken out of my sails I began to look for where we should go. I applied for several jobs but nothing worked out. I contacted my advisor at WSU and enquired about pursuing a doctorate degree. He offered me a paid assistantship on the spot and asked how soon we could get moved back to Pullman. So, with no work available and a fully paid doctorate with a monthly stipend available it was obvious this was where God was leading us. We packed up our few belongings and headed back to Pullman in the middle of a cold winter.

Grad School and Food Stamps

Pullman in January is usually sub-freezing nights and cold, windy days. This is what greeted us when we rolled into town one cold, snowy day in late January. We found a small 2 bedroom apartment off campus near an elementary school for the first few months we were in town. We eventually found a 3 bedroom duplex with a yard that went right into an elementary playground which we ended up staying in for the remainder of the 5 years we were in Pullman. When we arrived in town we were pretty much broke with no money so we applied for welfare assistance and food stamps. We felt much like the Cambodian refugees who we had helped in Tacoma. We did get assistance for a few months only to find out that we were denied further assistance because of a clerical error in the welfare office and we had to pay back all the money we had received. With welfare it doesn't matter whose fault it is for errors, the recipient is always responsible for repayment. Well, you can imagine our desperation seeing we were living on a shoe string and we now had to repay hundreds of dollars to the state for an error they made! They didn't care how much we paid each month so we set up a payment plan of $5 per month.

Cheerios and Chemistry

Graduate school was challenging and exciting. I enjoyed research because I was learning new things all the time and figuring out new areas where no one had researched before. My advisor was a great man, Ralph Cavalieri, who was also a Christian. We had a great working relationship and he challenged me a lot in my research. I ended up focusing my research on extrusion processing of cereal. This is a process that is used in the food industry to make shaped cereals like Cheerios or Lucky Charms. My research focused on studying the chemical reactions in the protein and starch of wheat during extrusion that gave the finished cereal its texture and structure with the hope of ultimately controlling the extrusion process to predict a cereal's final quality. It was a lofty goal which was not achieved but we learned a lot along the way. I ended up getting a second Master's degree in chemical engineering and then a doctorate in the same field. When we first moved back to Pullman to pursue a doctorate I thought I would be able to complete it in 3 years but it ended up taking 5 years. If I had realized I would be in college for over 10 years when I first started thinking about college back in Tacoma I would have never started. There were many times throughout my years in college where I thought I would never be done. It was during these college years that God changed my heart and my head about my role in missions.

How China Came to Our Doorstep

I made some great friends while in grad school. One of my office mates was from China and we got to be good friends. He taught me how to speak some Chinese and how to cook their food. One of the games we played when he came over to our house was a dice game we called Ten Thousand. He taught me how to count to ten thousand in Chinese while playing that game. Another office mate was from India. He was very smart and also very entertaining to listen to. He had a very strong accent and talked in English very fast so the combination made it difficult to understand him until you got used to his accent. Connie never did understand him so I ended up translating a lot of what he said when we would get together with him and his family. I was in my early thirties when I started graduate school. I was surprised how many other graduate students were our age and had families. We formed a close-knit group of friends who remain good friends today even though they are scattered all over the country.

The Blinders Are Slowly Coming Off

When we returned to Pullman for graduate school we went back to our old church. We explained to them what had happened with our plans of not going to China and where we felt we were now headed. The church had a different pastor when we returned to Pullman and his emphasis was much more on the believer than on missions, though he did support it and preach it. The emphasis was focused on becoming students of the Bible and learning how to dig out nuggets as diligent students instead of being spoon fed by the pastor. I came across passages in Genesis where it showed how God equipped men with specific skills for building the tabernacle. I also learned about men God used in governments and business to accomplish great things for Him. I also learned how significant our work is to God in and of itself. God is a worker (He worked on creation for six days and rested the seventh) and He has created us to work. I also learned that when I work and provide for my family it is an example of how God provides for us. God was slowly taking the blinders off of my eyes so that I could see the bigger picture. This didn't mean missions was not important to God and to His church, but His plans for each of us should be dictated by His leading and not by our pre-supposed ideas. I had finally come to the realization that God was leading me and our family into a life of working full time. It had taken over 5 years for God to change my head and heart.

Changing Course . . . Slightly

I changed my field of study in agricultural engineering to chemical engineering when I went back to grad school in 1988 since this would open up more job opportunities in the U.S. and still allow me to work in the food processing industry where a lot of chemical engineers work. I approached my advisor about changing my degree to chemical engineering once back in grad school and he was agreeable to the change since he was a faculty member in both the chemical and agricultural engineering departments. His degree was in chemical engineering and he understood my desire to go into this field because of its applicability to so many different types of jobs from petroleum to food to pharmaceuticals to energy. It was another example of how God was using my desire to go in a certain direction to accomplish His purposes in my life. He was leading through what some would say was just personal ambition but I happen to believe that God places desires in our lives that we many times think are our own. So, I decided to follow that desire to see where it would lead me.

Take This Job and Love It!

Networking My Way to a Job

It was a bleak job market as I was finishing up my Ph.D. in late 1993 and early 1994. Earlier in 1993 I went to a conference sponsored by the American Institute of Chemical Engineers (AIChE) in Seattle and met many representatives of companies who were there giving presentations. I had become a member of AIChE and bought a membership directory. This directory listed members by state and company. I used this directory to contact members who were going to be attending the AIChE conference in Seattle. I ended up having over half a dozen interviews with company representatives from 3M, GE, DuPont, Dow Chemical, CH2M Hill, Bend Research, and Westinghouse. Most of my colleagues from grad school were using the AIChE career fair held during the conference to get potential interviews but none of them even got any since most companies were not actively recruiting. When I told them about all my interviews they were amazed. None of my interviews resulted in any offers but it reinforced my conviction that jobs are found by actively networking and building relationships with real people, not how good a resume looks. I continued to use the membership directory as my primary job hunting method. I did a lot of cold calls using names from the directory and never experienced a rejection from the person I called. In almost all instances, when they learned I had got their name from the directory, they were very interested to help in any way they could. It was a cold call to a chemical engineer at the Kellogg Company in Michigan that ultimately resulted in my first engineering job. Another job offer came from Westinghouse in central Washington State at the Hanford reservation from a cold call from the membership

45

directory too. The Hanford job ended up falling through because of a hiring freeze. It ended up being a good thing that I didn't get the Westinghouse job because a couple of years after the offer they lost their contract with Hanford and everyone was laid off including the manager who wanted to hire me.

Kellogg's of Battle Creek

My interview trip to Michigan was a two-day event. My first day was scheduled with back-to-back interviews along with an hour presentation I gave on my Ph.D. research. I had dinner with some of the interviewers that first night. The second day was a half-day scheduled with tours of the Kellogg's research and development and production facilities and then a wrap up with a handful of the people I had met. There was not an immediate offer because they were interviewing multiple candidates and they said that I would hear back from them in a week or two. I got back on the plane that afternoon to head back to Pullman with a feeling that this was going to be the next place my family and I were going to be living. Sure enough, a week later I received a phone call from the hiring manager with a job offer. I said I would let him know my answer in a couple of days so I could talk it over with Connie and the kids before making a decision. We talked and prayed and prayed and talked some more over the next couple of days. With no other job offers on the table it became pretty clear that this was God's provision for our family. As with other previous major decisions in our lives we used the peace of God as our guiding principle. If we felt His peace about a decision, then we did it. If there was no peace, then we didn't do it. We based this out of the passage in Ephesians where Paul states, "Let the peace of God rule in your lives." The word "rule" in that passage is a similar word to mean being an umpire. Let the peace of God act as an umpire in making life's decisions. You don't have to make fleeces or ask for weird signs from God when making decisions. You just have to have His peace, that settled feeling, that sense that there aren't lingering doubts, an assurance that this "sits well" with us. Yes, you could say that this is very subjective and that it is based on feelings. Well, God has given us feelings for a reason and we should not be afraid of them. Obviously, if our feelings go against God given principles and morals then it is not the peace of God we are feeling. But if we cannot see an obvious moral issue with our decision and it "feels" good without lingering doubts or what some refer to as a "check in our spirit", then go for it. Is it fool proof? No. But you have to trust God at some point that He is leading you. We have made mistakes, but overall, we have seen His hand guiding us in our major life decisions using this principle.

I remember sitting in the hotel in downtown Battle Creek, Michigan, during my interview trip at Kellogg's. I had decided to interview with them even though I had a pending offer at Westinghouse just to see what an engineer does at a food company. One of the afternoons I was in the hotel I called Westinghouse to check on the job status and learned then that I would not get the job. It was a typical February day in Battle Creek: cold, snowy, and gray skies. Not a very inspiring setting to bring my family to. I was bummed. I really wanted the job at Westinghouse. I was not looking forward to moving to the Midwest. We liked the Pacific NW, had lived there all of our lives, and all of our family and friends lived there. But with the economic conditions of the mid-1990's we didn't have many options and having a good job in Michigan was better than no job in Washington State. So, with sadness of leaving our family and friends in Washington State and some excitement of the new adventure that lay ahead of us in Michigan, we packed our few things and moved back to Battle Creek.

None of us had ever been to Michigan before so we were glad that it was still going to be near a big body of water of Lake Michigan, but there were no mountains to speak of. There were some foothills in the northern part of the lower peninsula and in the UP (upper peninsula) of Michigan, but in Battle Creek the largest hills were those leading up to freeway overpasses! No mountains or hills whatsoever! There were a lot of lakes though. Michigan has over 10,000 small lakes besides the Great Lakes. I think God created Michigan that way because during the hot, humid summers you need a lot of water to stay cool. Our first summer in Michigan was a lesson in how to stay cool. It was hot and humid all summer. When we would get up in the morning and see the sun filtered by a very hazy sky and air around us we knew we were in for a humid day. The Pacific NW does not have the kind of humidity that the Midwest does. The Pacific Ocean acts like a natural air conditioner and we never experienced the humid conditions Michigan does during the summer. So, when we tried working outside in the yard or on outdoor house projects we learned quickly to pace ourselves so we didn't overheat.

Our First House

The housing market in Battle Creek and Michigan in general was much cheaper than the Pacific NW. We were able to buy our first house only a couple of months after moving there. Kellogg's paid all of our closing costs and we had been able to save up enough money for a down payment while in grad school. So, we were excited to finally own our first house. It was in an established neighborhood, had mature landscaping, and had been recently remodeled. We were able to get our first pets since being married. Connie took Leah and Luke to a local humane society and they each got a kitten. They were both in the same cage so they got both of them. One was a mainecoon

48

type looking cat and the other was short hair gray tabby cat. They kept the kids entertained that summer until they were able to make friends at school. We called the kittens Tom and Jeri.

Cereal Engineering . . . Really?

Work at Kellogg's was fun and fascinating. My first job was in product development where we worked on new and improved ready-to-eat breakfast cereals. There was a large pilot-scale facility that we worked in where we could run small batches of new and improved cereals without having to use the large production facilities and disrupt their production schedules.

It was fun working in the pilot plant and being able to eat your experiments! I remember working on a product improvement for a cereal called Product19. We were trying to increase the calcium claim in the cereal since the competitor's cereal had the higher calcium levels. When we increased the calcium level the cereal started to stick to the flaking mill. We worked weeks and weeks trying to figure out how to solve this seemingly simple problem. It was these kinds of projects that kept me interested in staying at Kellogg's but not in Michigan. One of the other things I liked about Kellogg's was their people and company culture. They had top-notch people and a team-based work culture that I really enjoyed. Every team had a camaraderie that was great. I got to know one of the technicians in the pilot plant who had worked at Kellogg's for many years. He was very knowledgeable on cereal and cereal processing. One day we were in the pilot plant and this technician was showing me how to operate a rotary pressure cooker where a lot of the corn grits were cooked prior to flaking them for cornflakes. When he found out I had a Ph.D. he laughingly pointed to the pressure cooker start button and said that Ph.D. meant "Push hear Dummy"! We both had a good laugh and kept on working. I think he appreciated my sense of humor and not taking myself too seriously as other Ph.D.s tend to do sometimes. We developed a great friendship during the 2 years I was at Kellogg's. Another interesting experience I had in the pilot plant was when another technician and I were running some test samples for a new product idea for India that had a lot of fiber content in it. It had the same active ingredient as Metamucil had and was a good dietary fiber source. We were running an extruder which can cook and form a cereal in one process step. If you have ever had Fruitloops, Lucky Charms, or other shaped cereals they are made using an extruder. It forces the cooked cereal dough out through a die which is the same shape you want the finished cereal to have. That particular day we were running this high fiber cereal and the technician was collecting samples coming out of the extruder in a plastic tub. We worked a couple of hours in the morning and I noticed that the technician was eating a lot of the samples and I warned him he better slow down or he would be hurting later from the adverse affects of too much fiber. Sure enough, a couple of hours later he went home with extreme gastro intestinal discomfort and didn't come back to work until the next day!

Cereal extruder

My second year at Kellogg's I worked in the advance research group which was housed at a separate site from the main manufacturing, product development, and pilot plant facilities. There were engineers, chemists, and food scientists working on some of the most advanced projects for product and process ideas 3-5 years out in the future. I really enjoyed this time at Kellogg's. I was one of their extrusion process experts for the company. I spent a lot of time trying to figure out how to improve the process from a material interaction perspective (how does the process change the material properties of the cereal) and how the process could be more easily scaled up from the pilot plant to production. When a product and process are scaled up from a pilot plant scale to production scale there are always problems due to higher production rates changing how the process behaves. Engineers and food scientists spend a lot of time trying to successfully scale up a new product from the pilot scale to production. The Holy Grail was to find some process parameters which could be used to more quickly scale up a process. Without those predictive parameters it was a trial-and-error process and always took a lot of time. We never did find a reliable set of parameters to aid us in scale up but that didn't stop us from continuing to try. One area that we learned a lot from was die design from the plastics industry for scale up. When an extruded cereal is forced through a metal die opening at the end of the extruder the final shape changes quite a bit from expansion when water is vaporized coming out of the extruder. The plastics industry had come up with a computer modeling program where a given die shape could be specified along with the material properties which were then used to try to predict the final product shape more accurately and reliably. Before having this computer program what we ended up doing was guessing the die shape, run some cereal through it, take the die plate off and tweak the shape in the machine shop and try it again until we got it right. This could take days of work. Once we got the die shape computer model we could many time get the shape estimated correctly the first time. It was a lesson to me of how to look at a different industry to see how to solve a similar but unrelated problem. One thing I was always cognitive of while at Kellogg's was the favor I had with my co-workers and management. I believe it was a result of God giving me favor with them as He had with Daniel and other biblical characters in their lives. I don't equate myself with Daniel and other biblical characters in stature or importance, but just as a child of God who is depending on Him for favor on the job, nothing more. It is still a walk of faith to depend on Him for provision of not only finances with our job but also for favor, expertise, and understanding which He can also provide.

The Oregon Trail

What Do Pop Tarts and Printers Have in Common?

I continued my job searching even after starting work at Kellogg's. Though I loved working at Kellogg's we missed our friends and family back in Washington State. I had applied to Hewlett Packard before applying to Kellogg's but had not heard any reply back from them. I had a colleague from grad school, Patrick, who did get a job with them at their San Diego site working on inkjet printers. I started a year and a half email conversation with him that eventually got me an interview with the inkjet division in Corvallis, Oregon. Patrick had worked with a manager in Corvallis on a project that lasted for 8 months. Patrick and the manager hit it off well, so when Patrick contacted this manager to see if he knew of any jobs, he told Patrick to have me send my resume to him. I sent the manager my resume in early fall of 1995. We exchanged emails several times and he always encouraged me to stay in contact with him and check in periodically to see what opportunities were available. We continued to exchange emails throughout the fall and holiday season. After the New Year in 1996 I contacted the manager again just to check in and he said that he was hearing of some possibilities in the next several months and encouraged me to stay in contact with him on a regular basis. In March of that year he sent my resume to a hiring manager who had a potential opening in a manufacturing group for making inkjet cartridges. In mid-March I had a phone interview with one of his experts. I knew from talking with Patrick that phone interviews at HP can be quite grueling so I was expecting the worst when I did have the phone interview. I spent weeks learning all I could about inkjet technology and manufacturing. When the day came for the phone interview the expert basically engaged in small talk for about 20 minutes and then asked me if I was interested in coming to Corvallis for an interview. I almost fell out of my chair! I was still expecting a grueling technical interview after the small talk ended, not an interview invite! So, after 30 minutes the interview was over, I had not had the grueling interrogation, and I was on my way to Corvallis for an interview in early April. I was excited, thrilled, amazed! Just a month before this phone interview I had received a sizeable raise at Kellogg's because they had recently learned how well other industries were paying chemical engineers and were afraid of losing me. I told Connie that no matter what HP would offer I would take it even if it was the same pay as at Kellogg's. I set up the interview date to coincide with the Easter holiday that Kellogg's gave us each year. We got both Friday and Monday off and many people took another day off to make it a five day weekend. Since my HP interview was scheduled for that Monday I decided to take Tuesday off too so that I could go out to Oregon on Sunday and return on Tuesday and no one would know I had left town! I flew out of the airport in Kalamazoo in a snow flurry which is not unusual for early April in Michigan. It was a short hop to Chicago where I caught my connecting flight to Portland, Oregon. Four hours later I flew into beautiful Portland under sunny skies and 70 degree weather. I picked up a rental car at the airport and drove the hour and a half 80 mile drive to Corvallis with the windows wide open enjoying the beautiful Oregon weather and scenery. When the plane was approaching Portland I could see the Columbia Gorge, Mt. Hood, and the mountains up the Cascades as far as Seattle where Mt. Rainier was clearly visible. I told God right then that I would really enjoy being back in the Pacific NW and would do anything to get back here. I asked Him again for His favor during the interviews on Monday and for favor with the hiring manager. From working at Kellogg's I realized that it is much more than how much knowledge and expertise one has in getting a job but also how well you "fit" into a company's culture and working group that is hiring you. So though I had done my homework about the technology I also wanted to learn about HP's culture and the people I might be working with. Monday was an all-day interview marathon starting at 8 am and going until 4 pm. It was actually less grueling than the interview trip I had with Kellogg's where it was a day and a half along with giving an hour presentation. I didn't have to give any presentation and I had only one day of interviews, but I was still exhausted at the end of the day due to the time change from Michigan, travel, and stress of the interviews. I felt that all of the interviews went well and that my last interview of the day with the hiring manager had gone particularly well. I could tell during the interview with the hiring manager that we were hitting it off well and that he liked me. I left HP that day to go back to my hotel with a lot of anticipation and excitement. The day had gone well, I liked what I saw, it was an exciting place to work, and it was in the Pacific NW. The next morning I got on my return flight back to Michigan telling God again that I would love to have this job and be back in the northwest. I got into Kalamazoo around dinner time and went back to work the next morning on Wednesday with none of my co-workers at Kellogg's ever suspecting I had been on an interview trip on the west coast. That following Sunday I got a call from the hiring manager at HP with an offer that far surpassed my expectations. They were offering me a twenty percent salary increase over my recent increased salary at Kellogg's. It was more in line with what engineers with my background and degree were getting in industry and it made me feel good. I didn't immediately accept the offer, though I knew I would, but said I would get back with him in a couple of days after talking it over with my family. Well, those couple of days of talking it over with the family were more of how fast could we get back to Oregon. I called the hiring manager back a couple of days later to accept his offer and negotiate a starting date. The offer came on Connie's birthday in mid-April and I negotiated a start date of June 17th so that we could wait until the school year was over before we had to move. I was surprised that they were willing to wait so long for me to start but after I had worked at HP for awhile I learned that this was not at all unusual and that many times they were willing to wait six months to a year for a good candidate. The next day after accepting the offer I gave my resignation at Kellogg's and asked if I could continue to work there until early June. Since I was going to a non-competitor company they were fine with it and encouraged me to work as long as I wanted. I gave such an early notice because I had a European business trip coming up at the end of April and I thought it would be bad form to go on such a trip and then immediately give my resignation after the trip was over. My manager at Kellogg's did ask me how I was able to go all the way to Oregon to interview with HP without anyone at Kellogg's knowing. He could never figure out when I had gone since I had done it over the Easter holiday. I think I would still be at Kellogg's today if they were on the west coast. I have nothing but fond memories of the people and culture at Kellogg's.

How to Sell a House in One Day and End Up In Oregon

We put the house up for sale the first week of May and had a full-priced offer the same day without any inspections required or other contingencies. It was the buyer from heaven. We closed on the place three weeks later and had the cash in the bank before leaving Michigan. We actually made money on the house after only owning it for about two years. It was another sign from God that He was leading us to Oregon. We had bought a minivan earlier that year and we drove to Oregon with the two cats and suitcases all crammed in together. HP gave us a budget for traveling which covered all of our expenses so we ended up turning it into a mini vacation. We stopped in Chicago, the Mall of America in Minneapolis, and Pullman where we had moved from two years earlier after finishing grad school. Connie and the kids had not seen Corvallis yet since we decided to wait until we moved to Corvallis to start looking for a house. HP put us in temporary housing for a couple of months while we looked for a house. It was a frustrating couple of months looking for affordable housing because the housing prices in Corvallis were much higher than in Battle Creek.

Corvallis, Oregon

We knew that west coast prices were higher than the Midwest but Corvallis had the highest prices in Oregon. HP had been in Corvallis over 20 years by the time I started working there but the inkjet business was ramping up very fast and they had hired thousands of people over a couple of year timeframe to keep up with demand. So, by the time we arrived at the peak of hiring in 1996 the housing prices had gone out the roof too. We bought a new house which was about half the square footage of our house in Michigan and about a third of the lot size for about fifty percent more in price. At first it was discouraging, but we accepted the fact that it wasn't going to change soon so we bought the place hoping that the housing prices would continue to increase so we could move up to a larger place in the future. The temporary housing HP put us up in was an apartment complex. We learned the hard way that there were a bunch of Irish HP employees staying in the same complex. I said we learned the hard way because after a few days in our apartment we were awakened in the middle of the night with loud music and a lot of laughter and loud talking in the apartment upstairs. We complained to the apartment managers. At work the next week I was complaining to some colleagues about the partiers and they said that they were most likely Irish employees being trained to transfer some manufacturing lines for inkjet printer cartridges to Ireland. We finally moved into our new house after 2 months of living in the apartments and started to figure out how to get rid of all the extra stuff that was packed into our garage.

It was great being back in the beautiful Pacific Northwest especially so close to the legendary Oregon coast. Oregon's 380 mile coastline is all public beaches and Highway 101 is one of the most scenic highways in the nation. We were only 55 miles from the coast in Corvallis so it took only about an hour to drive to Newport, one of the larger towns along the coast. Corvallis is home to Oregon State University with about 20,000 students. It is a great university town with a population of about 50,000 with a lot of cultural activities on campus ranging from plays to symphony concerts. We really enjoyed the summer outdoor community band concerts at the central park downtown. Every Tuesday evening during the summer months the community band held an hour long concert where everyone would bring a lawn chair, snacks, and a blanket to listen to great big band sounds under the stars. We immediately got involved with a local church, Westside Community Church, and they took us in and made us feel at home. They had a strong missions program along with a great worship team and many activities during the week. Our kids fit right in and it made our transition into Corvallis much easier and pleasant.

Inkjet Printers and the HP Way

HP's Corvallis campus was impressive. It was HP's consumer inkjet development center and it was situated on a 176 acre campus which was a former horse racing farm. It had over 2 million square feet of manufacturing and office space with over 7,000 employees and several thousand contractors. It was a small city in and of itself within the city of Corvallis. It was exciting being a part of such an enterprise responsible for over half of HP's profits at that time. What had started out as an idea by a few employees in the early 1980's had become a multi-billion dollar business by the time I arrived on campus 10 years later. The HP Way was a culture in which everyone is considered equal and valued. Even the most senior managers on site were in cubicles like the one I had. You could approach any manager no matter how high up they were with no fear of reprisal if you wanted to talk to them about something, either an idea or a complaint. It was an open door policy. Everyone also shared in the profits of the company. If the company did well, then everyone shared the profits, not just the CEO and upper management. Sadly, that has changed even at HP and there is no longer that profit sharing that the founders so strongly believed in and encouraged.

It was exciting to be a part of such a fast growing business and one felt you were just hanging on for the ride! The first year I was at HP I was involved in a product launch for an inkjet printer that was the first on the market for printing photos. The printer was an instant success and set HP up for the next few years as a market leader in photo printing. The program leader for the new inkjet printer took the entire product team out for a dinner cruise in Portland. There were several hundred employees who ended up going on the cruise. It shows how wildly successful HP was with these products and how the employees got to share in the success of it too. I initially worked as a manufacturing engineer responsible for a set of manufacturing processes used to make inkjet cartridges. I was responsible for making sure the processes were operating efficiently and also for continually improving the processes. Though I enjoyed research and development, or what is referred to as R&D, my time in manufacturing was a great experience which helped me a lot when I eventually did get into R&D. People in R&D without manufacturing experience don't realize many times how unrealistic their designs or ideas are because they don't understand what it takes to manufacture something. It might be a great idea, but impossible to manufacture easily or economically. I'm glad I got the manufacturing experience before going into R&D. When I first came to HP I was hoping to go directly into R&D, but God saw the bigger picture and the open door He provided was in manufacturing. So many times we think the way things turn out are just coincidence or chance, but in God's eyes He is orchestrating things so that it goes the way He wants. In retrospect, the manufacturing position was the best thing to prepare me for the next decade of work I would do for HP in R&D. God wants to be involved in our careers and, if we let Him, He will direct us into exciting and meaningful jobs and projects. I am continually amazed at how He has opened doors of opportunity for me at HP.

Around the World in 10 Days

I have traveled quite a bit for HP too. Travel was usually dictated by the project I was working on at the time such as a supplier or equipment vendor we needed. I also attended a lot of tradeshows and conferences. One project I had entailed working with a material supplier in Boston and I was able to travel there dozens of times. I got to know Boston pretty well and really liked the city. I used to give the people in Boston a bad time about rearranging the use of the letter "r". They would say "ca" for "car" and "idear" for "idea. I called it the conservation of "r's"! I also worked with another HP site in San Diego on a particular project where I had to go down there for a few days per month over a two year period. The site was in Rancho Bernardo about 20 miles northeast of downtown San Diego. I found a small, nice hotel on Coronado Island where I liked to stay because it was close to downtown and the water. It was an easy commute because I was going against traffic both ways. At one point we were actually considering transferring to the San Diego site but ultimately decided against it because real estate was so expensive. I was also the primary expert for a certain material HP used to assemble inkjet cartridges and I had to travel to all HP's offshore sites to train engineers on the material technology. I literally traveled around the world in ten days on one trip going to Singapore, Ireland, and Puerto Rico where all of our offshore manufacturing sites were located. Most recently I have been involved in developing some international standards which HP is interested in supporting so I have traveled to Berlin a couple of times and to Brazil once. There have been numerous other trips during my 16 years at HP so far and it would fill another chapter to describe all of them. I think God knew about my love of travel and so He has orchestrated my projects to allow me to do as much traveling as I have. God loves to fulfill our desires when we put Him first, honor Him with our love and commitment, and make Him a priority in our lives. What father doesn't want to lavish good things on their children when they honor him?

The Ultimate Vocation

By this time I had come to terms with what it means to take this job and love it. I had also come to terms about what God's ultimate purpose was for my life. I was meant to be an engineer for my life's vocation, not a missionary. It has not been an easy journey, but it has been a rewarding one. Sometimes it takes years to find that vocation like it did for me. For others it comes quickly and clearly. I don't regret the choices I have made, though it might have made my life a lot easier if I had realized what vocation God had for me earlier. God takes all of our choices whether good or bad and uses them ultimately to shape us into His image. He is not afraid of our mistakes, misconceptions, or unbelief. He is not insecure. He knows who is in control. We just have to come to that realization so we can allow Him to take control. It doesn't mean becoming a robot either. He wants us to freely love Him, not out of a legalistic dogma or belief system, but because we realize He created us for a relationship with Him. What has brought so much freedom to my life is realizing that when I am in a relationship with God I really have freedom to make choices about my life's work. It's not a legalistic thing but one of discovery and exploration. He's not afraid of the choices and decisions we make either. He gave us a free will and He expects us to use it. He has given us talents and skills that He wants us to use to bless our families and others.

Epilogue

It is approaching 20 years since I started down the path of working full time as an engineer. I could not have predicted back then where this career choice would lead me. It has been a rewarding and exciting profession to work in and there is no doubt in my mind that God directed my steps to work in this field. I have been involved in manufacturing, research & development, supply chain, material development, process development, environmental life cycle assessment, and material regulatory tracking. I have been granted eight patents on processes and systems that were developed to manufacture ink jet cartridges. I have interacted with some very smart and talented people from many universities such as MIT, Cal Berkeley, OSU, Rutgers, and my alma mater, WSU. I have worked with researchers at Battelle Institute, Pacific NW National Labs, and Southwest Research Institute. I have worked with colleagues from around the world. I have participated in industry working groups for standards and met people from all over the world. I have had the opportunity to give presentations at conferences and universities. It has been a full and rewarding 20 year career so far and I suspect the future will be the same. I have been working the last few years at HP in the environmental area. HP along with many other large corporations is grappling with how to make their businesses more sustainable and use the resources we have wisely. I have seen my career go full circle from product development to now looking at what we do with all these products once they have reached the end of their useful life and need to be disposed of. There are some exciting opportunities in this field and I am looking forward to the challenges that it will bring. We are never too old to learn new things and I have no plans on retiring any time soon! I see the gifts and abilities God has given to me and I want to continue to use them for as long as God sees fit to keep me on this earth.

This journey I have been on the last 20 years is not a unique one. I have met many other believers who feel the same way as I do about God leading them into exciting professional and trades careers. And most of them do it quietly and diligently, not seeking glory or recognition. If you cornered them, though, and asked them how they got to where they are you would hear a similar story as I have told you but maybe without the full-time ministry part at the beginning in most cases. You would hear stories full of passion for God and also passion for the career He led them into. None of them or me has ever given a testimony at church on how God has led any of us into our careers, though, and that needs to be told so other believers will hear and be encouraged in the work they have given most of their life and energy to. Getting the word out about the significance of our work and career is what motivated me to write this book. I trust it will motivate you to be more vocal about your life's work and share it with others.

My deepest desire is that you have been encouraged by reading about the journey I have been on and that it has in some small way changed how you think about your work and career and, more importantly, how God views your work and career. Our work is significant to God. He has created us to work. So . . . take your job and love it!

Large signposts along my journey (there were many small signposts but too many to list)—A signpost is a post bearing a sign that gives information, guidance and direction, shows the way to go:

1962-1966   Fascinated by many stories from missionaries when going to school at King's Garden elementary school. Got an erector set and started building things. Loved building model airplanes and ships. Built a working model of an elevator for science fair project. (Hmmm, seeing an early indicator here? **Sign post #1**) Started playing violin at age 8.

1967   Started my lifelong love of the guitar. Bought my first electric guitar at a yard sale for $5.

1969-1974   Played guitar in high school jazz band.

1976   Got my first high tech job at a aerospace electronics company in Everett, WA. (**Sign post #2**)

1976   Started planning and saving for bicycle tour around Europe.

1977   Arrived in Norway to start a 6 month trip traveling through Europe. First contact with YWAM in Germany.

1980   Attended YWAM training school in Tacoma, Washington. First short term missions trip into Canada. Connie let me know that this was only short-term (**Sign post #3**)

| 1981 | Short term missions trip to Saipan and Tinian in the Mariana islands north of Guam. |

| 1981 | Started local ministry and outreach to Cambodian and Laotian refugees in Tacoma. |

| 1982 | Short term missions trip to Hong Kong. Smuggled Bibles into southern China. |

| 1982-1985 | Continued Cambodian and Laotian refugee ministry while going to the local community college in Tacoma. Met professor from heaven (Purdue University) who encouraged me to think about going back to school and find a profession that could be used for gaining access to countries who did not allow missionaries into their country. (**Sign post #4**) |

| 1982 | Started back to school at local community college thinking I could finish an engineering degree in a couple of years! Twelve years later I finally finish college!! |

| 1985 | Transferred to Washington State University (WSU) in Pullman, Washington. I enjoyed college and did very well (**Sign post #5**) |

| 1987 | Completed Bachelor Degree in Agricultural Engineering. Started a Master's Degree in Engineering Science. |

| 1988 | Completed Master's Degree and moved back to Tacoma to work for a food processing company and |

prepare to go to China teaching English as a second language at a university.

1988   Tiananmen Square massacre stops plans for going to China. (**Sign post #6**)

1989   Went back to Pullman to pursue a doctorate degree in Chemical Engineering. I got a full ride on a research assistantship (**Sign post #7**)

1991   Completed a Master's Degree in Chemical Engineering.

1994   Completed doctorate degree. Got a job offer from Westinghouse at the Hanford nuclear reservation in Eastern Washington. A hiring freeze prevents getting that job. Got another job offer from the Kellogg's Company in Battle Creek, Michigan. Off to Michigan we go to engineer cereal! (**Sign post #8**)

1996-present Received a job offer from the Hewlett Packard Company's Inkjet Printer Division in Corvallis, Oregon. Off to Oregon we go to engineer inkjet cartridges! Have had great favor with management and colleagues (**Sign post #9**)

You might be suited for full time work if:

- You're really good at a skill or talent like rocket scientist or world renowned clothes designer
- You have had a re-occurring desire to work in a certain profession or trade that does not go away after the first initial emotional pull and the desire only grows over time
- God comes to you in a vision or dream and tells you to do it (this rarely happens!)
- Your parents tell you to go to college or else! (Listen to them—it just might be God telling you through them)
- You have a spouse who encourages you to get a job (this was my situation)
- You have a mentor or friend who encourages you to pursue a job, trade, or profession
- Your pastor or spiritual leader tells you not to go into full time work (just kidding—kind of . . . , I had a pastor tell me that once but my heart was saying otherwise, so be confident in your decisions)
- You do well in college or trade/vocational school and enjoy it (most of the time!)
- You do well in your job and find favor with your boss and colleagues

You might be suited for full time ministry if:

- You enjoy meeting the needs of others
- It is a desire that doesn't go away with time
- Others encourage you to pursue full time ministry
- You have no interest or desire to work in a trade or profession, it just doesn't "click" with you
- God comes to you in a vision or dream (again, this rarely happens!)
- Your spouse, family, and friends support your decision to be in full time ministry

You might be suited for being a tentmaker if:

- You have a skill or profession that can be used overseas
- You enjoy cross-cultural experiences
- You enjoy natural contact with people through your job
- You want to reach the unreached
- You want to integrate your faith & work
- You want to use your education and experience
- You want to earn a salary—no fundraising necassary

Additional books on the topic:

"Your work matters to God", Doug Sherman and William Hendricks, NavPress 1987

Why I Left World Vision and Went into Finance, Mark Sheerin http://www.christianitytoday.com/thisisourcity/7thcity/why-i-left-world-vision-for-finance.html

"Work Matters: Connecting Sunday Worship to Monday Work", Tom Nelson, Crossway Publishing 2011

"Work Matters: Lessons from Scripture", R. Paul Stevens, Eerdmans Publishing Company 2012

"Every Good Endeavor: Connecting Your Work to God's Work", Timothy Keller, Penguin Group 2012

"God at Work", Gene Edward Veith Jr., Crossway Publishing 2002

"Work: A Kingdom Perspective on Labor", Ben Witherington III, Eerdmans Publishing Company 2011

About the author:

Tim has worked at the Hewlett Packard Company for over 17 years in research and development, product development, and most recently in environmental compliance. He holds 8 patents and has been involved in several start-up companies. Tim and his wife, Connie, live in Portland, Oregon. They have two grown children and 2 grandchildren. They have lived in the Pacific Northwest most of their lives and spent a majority of that time living in the Puget Sound area of Everett and Tacoma before moving to Oregon 17 years ago. Connie has a small cereal start-up company selling specialty granolas. In their spare time they enjoy spending time with their family, landscaping and gardening, and music.